Charles Norman

THE HORNBEAM TREE
and Other Poems

Illustrated by Ted Rand

HENRY HOLT AND COMPANY · NEW YORK

Chickadees

The feeder is a hive;
These bees are chickadees,
Alighting with fat feet
From bare or budding trees,
Black-capped, black-bibbed, white-cheeked,
Like clowns on a trapeze.

Now they put on their act
Of undulating flight,
Tobogganing on air
And glancing with delight
At the one standing there
Enraptured at the sight.

The Belted Kingfisher

The Kingfisher is curious,
He rattles when in flight;
His eyes are big, his furious
Look can give a fright,
Especially over water
When he spots a fish below
And dives bill first to snatch it
Where it doesn't wish to go.
The fish looks up—it is too late,
The Kingfisher has sealed its fate.

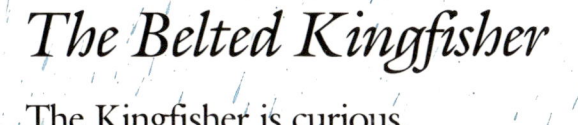

Hairy and Downy: Woodpeckers

Two birds there are that look alike
In everything except their size:
See the Downy—it is small;
Here comes Hairy—a surprise!
The same bird in a larger guise.
The same red bar behind his head,
The same black tail, the same white back,
In front the same old white and black.
How to tell one from the other?
Hairy has a longer bill—
To be expected in a bird
That's bigger though identical.

The Cardinal

Lordly and aloof,
A cardinal on a locust bough
Tries not to look conspicuous
In red, but doesn't quite know how.

Condescending to descend,
The feeder being clear
Of little, chattering chickadees,
He pecks genteelly, no one near.

Another cardinal, in flight,
Thinking to take pot luck with kin,
Approaches after changing course,
Is met head-on while gliding in.

Stiff wings and jabbing beak
Greet him before he can alight;
He hovers, tries to swerve, to rise,
Escapes bedraggled, showing fright.

The first returns to his repast,
Is once more pecking daintily.
Survival of the fittest, yes;
Alarming all the same to see.

Different Feathers

People look like other people,
Dogs look like people,
And now look: squatting on a stump,
A phoebe looking like a frump.

But the petite wren
Is quite another hen;
Her work is never done,
Yet she is always cheerful,
As well as attractive,
And sings often, without much of an ear.

Now the goldfinches glide in
Like rich folks in a limousine;
Nobody molests them,
They are so elegant,
Slumming among the flowers.
But a catbird by the lilac bush,
Dark, handsome, villainously slim,
Cocks a calculating eye.

There, half hidden by the grass,
Is a chipping sparrow.
O you redhead!
You remind me of someone I once knew,
Who was almost as little as you.

As for the robin at this time of year,
Twanging the yanked, reluctant worm,
Commuting from the apple tree where he nests
To the cherry tree where he feasts,
Taking a peck at the catbird while in flight,
Just to give him a good fright,
What with clamorous young,
And a living to get,
He's also lean and trim.
See him standing still,
All line, like something carved
By a Pennsylvania Dutchman
Tired of making decoy ducks.

The Nuthatch

The nuthatch, when it climbs a tree,
Creeps left and right diagonally.
That's odd, of course; but, odder still,
On coming back the way it went,
Once more on the diagonal,
It makes an upside-down descent.
"Who, who, who" it nasally sings,
Tail pointing up to higher things.

The Hornbeam Tree
at Merrillton

Inside the house the hornbeam made
Summer slept in leafy shade;
But suddenly a wind was there
That did not come from anywhere,
The leaves fell silently as snow;
The woodland paths began to flow
In watercolor streams, and then,
Trees turned into twigs again.

A Parlement of Swallows

"Where did they come from?" my wife asked;
I said from all the barns about
And all the barns from here to Maine.
A thousand swallows perched on wires,
Then rose as though there'd been a shout,
And so became a thousand specks
Like pepper sprinkled in the sky
By a tall genie of the air.
A thousand specks returned as birds,
Or notes or staves of music there,
To that assembly place of wires.

The sky was now an empty blue,
But soon some distant blurs showed through
Like commas and quotation marks,
Then swallows heading for the sea;
With scissoring tails they came and came
And took their places on the wires
As far as all the wires went,
To join the swallows' parlement.

"Where are they going?" my wife asked.
I said to winter in Brazil,
And to myself at summer's end
To winter in my thoughts until
The long New England winter ends.

Chickadees in Winter

The little clowns of spring,
Who have been God knows where,
Appear as though invoked
From the cold air.

It is a masquerade
Of white-cheeked pierrots,
Who bow and scrape,
And turn upon their toes.

Their beady eyes burn bright
To see the banquet laid—
The roof removed,
The seeds cascade.

White upon white the trees
Throng the whiter ground;
Stillness stretches white,
A woodland without sound.

The Snail

Of course his pace is rather slack,
He lugs a house upon his back;
Outside, when slithering about,
He lifts his small round head and face,
His eye-stalks wave, then stiffen out,
Just like a visitor from space;
He leaves behind a shining track.

A relative, the Banded Snail,
Is like a fish from head to tail;
Its yellow shell with bands of black,
Some thin, some wide,
Looks much too small
To hold it all
Should it decide
To go inside.

A Squirrel

Between our house and the trees
A squirrel with bowed head
And paws crossed on his breast
Begs for his daily bread.

Standing there he seems
A monk by his attire,
A white robe to his feet
Like a little White Friar.

Hello small friend I say,
With other welcoming words,
Here's bread to carry back
To your house of leaves and birds.

Deer on a Summer Day

As I came through the fields today
Grasshoppers flew up like spray;
The summer hum of heavy bees
Rang in the meadows of the air,
Until I reached a stand of trees
And saw the still deer standing there,
Five deer that stared in mild surprise
With the camera of their eyes.
Beautiful and statue-still,
They looked at man without ill will,
Then shook their sheaths of air,
And were no longer there.

The Woodchuck

The woodchuck is a sleepy beast;
He sleeps all winter through, at least;
In spring he gives his eyes a blink,
And trundles out to eat and drink.

"Aha!" he thinks, as woodchucks do,
"There seems to be a lot to chew;
So many leafy shoots and sprouts—
How nice the world is hereabouts!

So many stems festooned with green—
It's certain that I won't be seen;
I'll try a bit here, if you please—
Aha! That's good! What bliss! What ease!"

Delightful creature! It is sad
That, to be honest, I must add
Gardeners and farmers see
The woodchuck very differently.

The Beaver, Alas

The long-locked European came
And found the beaver, sleek and fat,
Shoring up the New World's leaks;
He did not see dexterity;
He saw the beaver as a hat.
Consider, children, carefully
This lesson in man's history:
All those battles in the woods,
That clash of empires fraught with fate,
And other like momentous matters,
Brought beaver hats to every pate,
And wealth and joy to all the hatters.

A Pride of Chipmunks

The littlest chipmunk of them all
Preens upon the garden wall;
He's small enough to be a mouse,
And live inside a cozy house,
But that's not where he's to be found;
When tired from his outdoor labors,
He much prefers a hole in the ground
To inconveniencing his neighbors.

One day I also saw his pa,
Although it could have been his ma;
They say two lions are a pride—
Here were two chipmunks, side by side,
A sire and his cub who dreamed,
So tawny, sleek and indolent,
A pride in miniature they seemed,
Or lions on a monument.

The Duckbilled Platypus

To be believed,
You must see it whole:
In front it's a duck,
Behind it's a mole.

In Australia,
Where you can get near,
They call it duck-mole,
Which makes it all clear.

The Sloth

Slothful the sloth
Is certainly noth;
When understood
His habits are good.
He never lies down,
But then never stands;
He hangs from a branch
By his feet and his hands,
Eating leaves by the peck
Right up to his neck.
Suspended with ease
From his leafy trapeze
He takes a long nap
Without fear of mishap.

Awake, quite refreshed,
He moves with great skill
To another lush branch
To get a refill;
It may take a while,
But that is his style;
He was made to be slow,
Not to gambol below;
He hangs as before,
And asks nothing more.
Who says that the sloth
Is slothful? He's noth.

At the Zoo

The whiskered seals
Looked moist and cool
As they slithered in
And out of their pool.

The kneeling camels
Chewed like cows;
The macaws cacawed
Under the boughs.

The shaggy yak
Showed his back.

The polar bear
Didn't care
Who stopped to stare;
He slept with his paws
Up in the air.

A Medley of Dogs

Spaniels are always nice to meet—
Those shaggy coats! Those fleecy ears!
Periscope tails and hairy feet,
Corduroy grins and moisty leers.

Bassets, who travel near the ground,
Are such a melancholy hound.
Their mournful eyes! Their ears like bags!
Which the sorrowful basset drags.

The poodle, on the other hand,
Prances like a fairy prince,
On ankles that are truly grand;
But anything can make him wince.

The lowly dachshund, sleek and sagging,
Is somewhat longer than he's tall;
His underside is always dragging,
But he's the cuddliest dog of all.

Of course, I don't insist on that;
Who knows, you may prefer a cat;
And if you do, I shall not mind,
For all who love a cat are kind.

for
Tom and Marcella

Library of Congress Catalog Card Number: 87-12033
Library of Congress Cataloging-in-Publication data is available.

ISBN: 0-8050-0417-3   First Edition

Printed in Japan
1 3 5 7 9 10 8 6 4 2

ISBN 0-8050-0417-3